Market ROMANTICISM

Market ROMANTICISM

A Consumer Romance Framework

The Concept Primer

TELECOMS EDITION

SHRIVATSAN BALAGOPAL

www.marketromanticism.com

Dedication

In loving memory of my father, G. N. Balagopal,
whose wisdom and values continue to guide me.

Publishing Support by Neutral Platforms Pvt Ltd
First Floor, Olympia Cyberspace, SIDCO Industrial Estate, Guindy, Chennai, 600032, TN, India

Author : Shrivatsan Balagopal
Year of Publication: 2025
Paperback ISBN: 978-93-344-5030-9
Digital ISBN: 978-93-344-4551-0

www.marketromanticism.com

CONTENTS

List of Figures:

List of Acronyms:

BAU: Business-as-usual

CPaaS: Communication Platform as a Service

B2B: Business– to– Business

OTT: Over The Top

B2B2C: Business–to– Business– to– Consumer

B2C: Business– to– Consumer

SoW: Share of Wallet

YoY: Year on Year

SIM: Subscriber Identity module or Subscriber Identification module.

RMS: Revenue Market Share

CVM: Customer Value Management

VAS: Value added services

ARPU: Average Revenue Per user

CRS: Consumer Romance Score

CLTV: Customer Lifetime Value

ROI: Return on Investment

CCaaS: Contact Center as a Service

AI: Artificial Intelligence

WISP: Wireless Internet Service Provider

FWA: Fixed Wireless Access

PREFACE

Checking the customer pulse is a **business-as-usual (BAU)** activity for a product manager or marketer. I was managing a product called **CPaaS (Communication Platform as a Service)**, a product within the **Business Communication** portfolio. It is a telecom solution designed for the enterprise segment **(B2B)**, intended to be sold to businesses (enterprise customers). CPaaS enables the businesses (brands) to engage with their end customers through omnichannel communication, and facilitates two-way interaction between the brand and its customers.

While I was analyzing the consumer perception and behaviour in the market for CPaaS, to develop a proactive product strategy and also to focus on omnichannel offerings to build required and appropriate partnerships , the market scan revealed an insight highlighting the changing landscape. I gathered a few data points on consumers' **preference** and **trust levels**. It was interesting to capture the changing consumer perception through these parameters. The activity was aimed to understand the consumer perception between **traditional channels (Voice** and **SMS)** and **OTT** based communication channels. The exercise does not limit to only the communication channels but also to understand what is shaping the market and how the landscape is evolving.

Later, while presenting the deck to my management stakeholders, there was a debate within the team whether preference and trust are the same or different. So I decided to clarify and said

> ***"I may like (prefer) a girl, but if there is a lack of trust, it will not lead to a relationship (commitment)."***

This analogy illustrated that **preference** reflects **liking or attraction**, whereas trust is critical for **commitment or action**. Hence **both** are **not the same**. This further piqued my research curiosity, which led me to come up with the concept **"Market Romanticism: A Consumer Romance Framework"** and to develop a full-fledged framework.

This edition focuses on the **telecom industry**, where the framework was first derived and applied for a telco & tech product. However, the concept has potential applications across technology and other industries, depending on feasibility, and is not limited to telecom.

The intended publication of this **Concept Primer** is to introduce the concept of **Market Romanticism** to the world—particularly to product managers, product marketers, and Product strategists in the telecom industry (though not limited to them). Academia may also find this framework relevant within marketing disciplines and could directly utilize it for teaching in business schools.

This primer serves as an introductory publication to the **forthcoming playbook** on **Market Romanticism**.

Hence, **The Concept Primer.**

INTRODUCTION

This concept was first derived and applied in the **B2B enterprise segment** of the **telecom industry**, particularly in **Business communication** products, i.e., **Communication Platform as a Service (CPaaS)**. While its initial application was in CPaaS, the framework is not limited to this product and can be applied across various business communication solutions, B2B products, and enterprise segments. I applied this concept to the CPaaS product, which was a live product with active usage and consumption, for which an analysis of **OTT based communication channels** and the development of an **omnichannel strategy** were required.

Additionally, the framework can extend beyond B2B into B2C or retail contexts, depending on the specific case and its adoptability. The concept can be applied to the **relationship** between a **consumer and a brand, or a consumer and a product**, in **B2B, B2B2C** and **B2C** contexts.

To provide readers with a clear understanding of the key concepts covered in this Concept Primer, definitions and explanations are presented upfront before engaging with the full framework.

Market romanticism is a study on **consumer-product** relationship and the competition's influence on this relationship and the product. Using an **analogy to a college romance**, the concept compares the **consumer-product relationship** to a **romantic relationship**, with **competitors** acting as a **third-party situation** in the relationship. The concept consists of two key aspects:

- **Consumer Romance:** A concept, measures consumer perception by understanding the stages of the romance. The metric **'Gossip level'** is introduced to quantify **Preference, Trust and Consumption levels**, directly relating to the Attraction, Trust and Commitment stages in the romance.

- **Consumer's Affair:** A concept to understand a firm's **SoW (Share of Wallet)** in a consumer with the **Relationship level** and **Intimacy Level**. (Read the concept for understanding).

The **Consumer romance** part deals with the **consumer perception**, and together with the **consumer's affair**, it addresses the overall **consumer behaviour.**

This concept is created with framework and metrics to understand the consumer behavior which helps and leads to carry out **Market Romanticization**.

Market Romanticization is a **Strategic plan** carried out, derived from the **insights of the study** (Market Romanticism) to **'win the heart'** of the consumer by:

- Attracting them,
- Understanding the Gossip level,
- Maintaining the desired Relationship level status,
- Increasing the consumer-product's Intimacy level, and
- Managing the Engagement mode.

Ultimately this concept helps in *formulating the effective product strategy by understanding shifts and evolution in the market landscape.*

MARKET ROMANTICISM : A CONSUMER ROMANCE FRAMEWORK

– The Concept Primer

THEORY

Similar to the stages of the buyer's journey — i.e. Awareness, Consideration, and Purchase (or Decision), extending to Retention and Advocacy — *which evolved from early decision-making models such as Lewis's (1898) AIDA framework and Engel, Blackwell and Miniard's (1995) Consumer Decision Process,* **I map consumer perception by inferring three key elements (or Levels) that explain how a consumer views or perceives** a specific product:

A. Preference level,
B. Trust level, and
C. Consumption level.

ANALOGY : A is seeing B (A sees B) Remember the undergraduate years? Gossip used to spread about our classmates that **"they both are seeing each other."**

This analogy forms the foundation for deriving and formulating the Consumer Romance Framework.

1. **A is attracted to B.**
   Meaning: The consumer is attracted to the product; hence, preference exists.

2. **A is attracted to B, but trust in B is low, so A isn't getting into a relationship.**
   Meaning: The consumer does not trust the product enough to use it yet.

3. **A is attracted to B, also trusts B, and is in a relationship with B.**
   Meaning: The consumer is committed to the product, which denotes the consumption or usage of the solution or service offerings.

A **survey** can be conducted on how consumers perceive the brand, based on the **three key elements: preference level, trust level,** and **consumption level.** I call this the **'Gossip Level'.**

A set of **pre-validated questionnaires** can be used in **surveys,** and secondary research data can also help analyze whether these levels are increasing or decreasing. The preference level, trust level, and consumption level can be benchmarked, and **trend analysis** can be captured **Year over Year (YoY).**

An extension of the **"Consumption Level"** is the **"Consumer's Affair"** concept, which adds depth to understanding the **Share of Wallet (SoW).** This helps in understanding the third-party situation by analyzing the influence of competitor products on the consumer–product relationship.

Example, A consumer uses two service providers or SIMs, SIM 'A' and SIM 'B'.

- Which service provider does the consumer use the most?
- What makes the consumer like both providers?
- How is each service being used?
- How often does the consumer use both SIMs?
- How well is each provider serving the user?
- What are the lean and peak usage periods for both SIMs?

This analysis also helps in understanding a firm's **Revenue Market Share (RMS).**

Any churn behavior first impacts the Usage revenue of a consumer, which is a subtopic but also a critical area when analyzing churn particularly in **CVM (Customer Value Management)**. There are three key areas to monitor:

1. **Usage Revenue:** Reduced usage or declining usage revenue may indicate weakening preference, signaling the start of a potential "affair" with competitors.

2. **Total Revenue (Usage + Rental + VAS, etc.):** A decline in the customer's overall ARPU (Avg Revenue Per User) due to plan changes or tariff reduction requests. This represents another inflection point in the consumer–product relationship.

3. **Total Revenue:** Nil Revenue: When total revenue from the customer drops to zero, it indicates churn, analogous to a "break-up."

These are the **inflection points** to capture in consumer behavior, caused by third-party situations (i.e., a consumer's affair – external factors) or compatibility issues (internal to the product) when trying to win the heart of the consumer in Market Romanticization.

- **Preference** and **trust** directly impact **consumption**.

- The **decrease** or **increase** in the **preference, trust**, or **consumption**, has its own **implication**.

The **levels of relationship** ***(Relationship Level)*** can be inferred from the following elements based on consumer behavior analysis:

- Loyal: Sticking to one product.

- Extra Affair: Using both products (liking both).

- Divorce or Break-up: Customer churn due to lack of trust or preference.

- Patch-up: Possibility to win back a customer based on efforts. A patch-up occurs when a previously lost customer is successfully won back.

Sometimes, a **divorce (customer churn)** may even result in a kind of **"alimony"** for the firm. This highlights the importance of returning to the basics—meeting the customer's expectations. If a person does not treat their partner properly, it can lead to **divorce (or break-up),** which in the business context means churn, and sometimes comes with an **"alimony"** cost.

Alimony in business terms can be understood as the **compensatory cost a firm** incurs after a customer churns. It can be both tangible and intangible.

- **Tangible alimony** includes refunds, waivers, non payments (bad debts) and Penalties

- **Intangible alimony** includes indirect and direct reputational damage, goodwill depletion, and brand trust erosion.

The Relationship Level with a customer can be maintained or enhanced through **appropriate Intimacy**, referred to as the **Intimacy Level**. Together, the **Relationship** and **Intimacy levels** constitute the **consumer's affair**.

This Market Romanticism concept can be applied to various scenarios, such as (i) New product development and launch, (ii) Understanding existing product consumption, and (iii) Analyzing evolving or changing consumer behavior and market landscape.

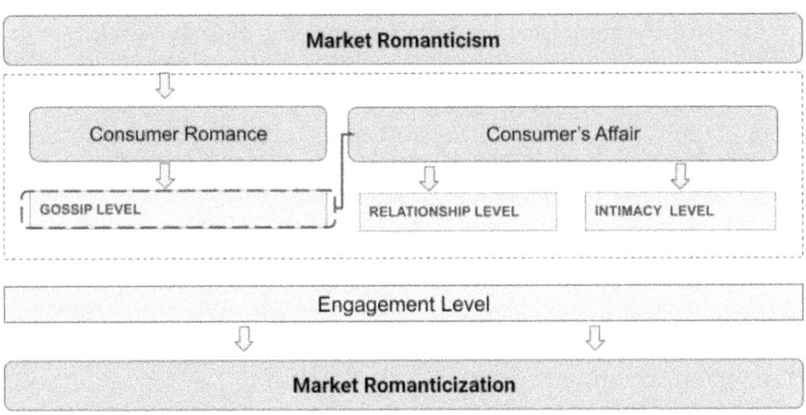

Figure 1.1 Market Romanticism framework – Diagram

To summarize as an abstract, Market Romanticism is structured as follows: Consumer Romance and Consumer Affair.

1. Consumer Romance – Gossip Level

- ❑ **Gossip Level**
  - Preference (Attraction)
  - Trust (Consideration)
  - Consumption (Relationship)

2. Consumer Affair – Relationship Level and Intimacy Level

- ❑ **Relationship Level:**
  - Loyal
  - Affair
  - Divorce or Break-up
  - Patch-up
  - Impact of Divorce: May sometimes lead to "alimony." It is essential to understand and analyze customer expectations to prevent churn. Meeting the customer expectation is essential and moderating the customer expectation effectively is key.

- ❑ **Intimacy Level:**
  - Emotional: Customer's willingness to endorse, provide testimonials, etc.
  - Bonding: Joint activities, programs, or events conducted with your customers. How often do you engage with your customers?
  - Mind Share: Opportunities for cross-sell, up-sell, VAS subscriptions, etc.
  - Nurturing: Rewards, cashbacks, rebates, or other incentives to motivate and strengthen the relationship.

- **Engagement Mode:** The firm's engagement, as an engagement mode (mode of interaction) between consumer and the product can be categorized as one of the following types of relationships:

A. Legally recognized union or Formal marital relationship ***(Marital union)***– i.e. **Marriage**

B. ***Cohabitation*** or cohabiting partnership **(Unmarried)**– i.e. **Living Together**

C. **Non-committed** relationship – i.e. **No Strings Attached**

When we look at engagement modes through the lens of billing, they can be compared to different types of relationships. The following analogy describes different engagement modes in terms of billing:

- If a **contract** and commitment are made with a consumer, it's like a marriage.

- If it's a **monthly subscription**, whether prepaid or postpaid, it's like living together

- If the payment model is **pay-as-you-go or pay-per-use**, it's like a "no strings attached" relationship.

We can further define the engagement mode in different ways, based on the models a firm adopts on a case-by-case basis. As shown in Figures 1.1 and 1.2, the engagement mode is represented separately in the diagram. The reason and logic for this is that it acts as an anchor, binding together Romance, Relationship, and Intimacy. Furthermore, the engagement mode is and must be a strategic choice under a product or brand's discretion, defining its customer engagement from a sales perspective.

Note: The **Relationship Level** refers to the **level of relationship**, whereas the **types of relationship** in the **engagement mode** are **distinct** and should not be confused. Both represent **different dimensions** within the framework.

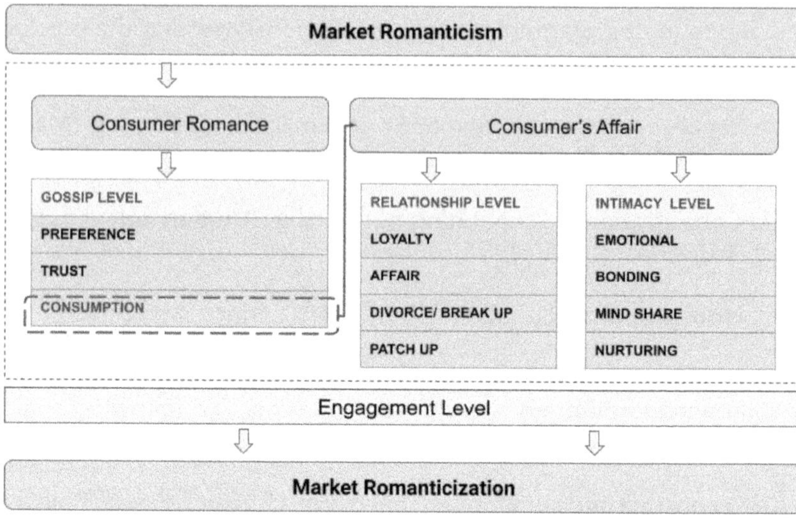

Figure 1.2 Market Romanticism framework – Detailed diagram

SCORE

Consumer Romance Score (CRS): The Consumer Romance Score (CRS) represents the metric for the **Gossip Level** only.

A guide to quantify the score:

- ❑ Based on the above metrics, a **weighted composite score** can be used to calculate the Consumer Romance Score (CRS) for a **product, brand**, or **category**. Each level can carry a specific weight to help quantify its business impact.

- ❑ A **pre-validated questionnaire** should be used to conduct **surveys** for measuring the **Gossip Level.**

- ❑ Appropriate survey methodologies can then be applied to analyze the **Relationship Level** and **Intimacy Level** to quantify the **consumer's affair.**

Note: *From the concept, it can be inferred that the term **'The Levels'** denotes **' The Levels of Consumer perception and behaviour'** which is detailed in the consumer romance and consumer's affair.*

PRACTICAL APPLICATION OF MARKET ROMANTICISM

This concept helps in understanding consumer perception and market dynamics, specifically how consumers interact with or perceive your product, and how competition influences their behavior.

Based on these insights, strategic actions can be planned to:

- ❑ Increase Share of Wallet (SoW) and market share.
- ❑ Take corrective actions in stages, levels, or areas where performance is lagging.

For example, as stated earlier in the preface and introduction, Initially I was deriving an omnichannel strategy to doubledown on OTT channels alongside the traditional channels. By analyzing consumer trust levels in traditional channels versus OTT, and studying trends in the Gossip Level, it was possible to derive actionable insights from the question:
"What is the consumer's perception?"

Initially the concept was applied to understand channel dynamics; later its application extended beyond the channels as a **strategic** tool to analyze from both marketing and strategy standpoint. The concept also informs **acquisition strategies** and **churn prevention (retention) strategies**.

For example, The **Leaky Bucket Theory (Ehrenberg, 2000),** coined by **Andrew Ehrenberg,** provides a useful comparison. Imagine a bucket where water is added at the top, but leaks from the bottom. Addressing these leaks is crucial for preventing customer churn.

The Market Romanticism independently addresses the challenge through its levels of Consumer Romance
and Consumer's Affair.

- ❑ **Consumer Romance:** Helps in **acquisition**, adding more water to the bucket.
- ❑ **Consumer Affair:** Provides **insights** into retention, churn prediction, and consumer behavior, helping to address the leaks.
- ❑ **Intimacy Level:** Ensures the water remains in the bucket, **creating stickiness** and **nurturing** the **consumer-product relationship**.

The key focus is on **monitoring** the **consumption Level** (Usage & Revenue report), because variations in consumption, whether increases or decreases, have a direct impact on revenue.

Thus, 'Market romanticism: A consumer romance framework' helps in understanding consumer perception and behaviour, applying it at both the product and brand contexts, using the levels as metrics.

Using the Levels for Strategy

- ❑ **Gossip Level:** Helps product managers or marketers identify which areas require focus and improvement to plan an effective strategy in **winning the customer.**

- ❑ **Relationship Level:** Reveals where the product excels or falls short, helps to **optimize** the **relationship** with the consumer and ultimately **optimize the consumption level.**

- ❑ **Intimacy Level:** Helps to **increase the stickiness,** build long-term consumer loyalty, generating top-of-mind awareness, mind share, better retention, churn prevention, increased **Share of Wallet (SoW),** higher **Customer Lifetime Value (CLTV),** and ultimately improved **Revenue Market Share (RMS) and Return on Investment (ROI).**

I applied this proprietary technique, "**Market Romanticism: A Consumer Romance Framework"**, to analyze **evolving consumer behaviour** and **monitor shifts** in **market** dynamics. This enabled me to proactively define both **"what now"** and **"what next"** in the **differentiation** game—particularly critical in a price-war-prone market. Moreover, and first and foremost, the framework helps in **staying relevant in the market**. To challenge and lead, the products and services must be relevant in the market.

For example, In India's **Communication Platform as a Service (CPaaS)** market, perception and trust levels are key parameters to observe between legacy channels such as Voice and SMS, and newer OTT-based communication channels. While Voice and SMS were once the only channels, the Indian market has witnessed a marked shift in favour of OTT channels, with their trust and adoption levels rising sharply. This trend is also true in a few regions globally.

This evolution is not merely anecdotal—it can be validated through an analysis of **revenue trajectories, churn behaviour, usage intensity**, and **adoption curves** across channels. Such data-driven insights can inform strategic decisions on where to differentiate. When it is said that OTT is favoured, the reliability and importance of traditional channels is not being discounted. In fact the term ' omnichannel' includes both traditional and OTT channels together. The intention is to provide a solution that enables brands or businesses to reach their end customers or for the consumers to reach their brands, where they prefer and engage most.

Note: *Preference and adoption patterns differ from consumer to consumer and from region to region globally.*

By analysing the magnitude of preference and trust levels, using the 'Levels of consumer perception and behavior', how can we strategize a differentiated offering through the adoption of OTT channels?

For example, a firm with a strong **moat**—such as entrenched **relationships** in specific **industry verticals** classified in its **account segments**—could leverage OTT as a **growth driver**, building unique service propositions anchored in the firm's **existing account base** to offer **differentiated offerings** for **specific use cases** on top of the specific **OTT based communication channels**. Specific **business operations** can be carried out on the **preferred OTT channels**, with **fall back communications** on other channels.

CONCLUDING NOTE

The telecom industry is regulated globally. The Indian telecom industry, however, remains one of the most regulated in the world.

Here, three forces continually **shape** industry direction:

1. Consumer behaviour,

2. Technology innovation, and

3. Regulations.

I call it **Market Shapers (Shapers of the industry)**. It is deliberate in the AI era, Technology innovation is a **critical macro factor as a shaper**. Particularly for business communication products i.e., CPaaS and CCaaS, where conversational AI has become an integral essential part of the business communication.

These ***shapers*** *are deeply* ***interlinked:*** *Consumer behaviour* ***dictates*** *adoption and usage patterns; Technology innovation* ***influences****, and is* ***influenced by****, these behaviours; and together they often* ***trigger*** *regulatory responses—ranging from new mandates to amendments.*

In such a landscape, where shifts happen, the Market Romanticism concept and framework help in analyzing the **changing landscape** and **consumer behaviour**. The Concept Market Romanticism enables a **product manager**, **marketer**, and **product strategist** to **analyze, track** and **differentiate** proactively. It also helps in understanding the consumer perception and behaviour, benchmark the Levels, reason out the metrics and analyze the key drivers behind the quantified scores. It further enables **identification of focus areas**, the **evolution of the landscape**, or **market shifts**, and **highlights which shapers** are **active** in a **specific industry** causing these changes. Ultimately, it **supports** the **creation** of a **strategic plan** for both **"What now"** and **"What next"**.

The Levels metric helps quantify both the consumer romance and the consumer's affair with a product. The reasons behind the score as a result of the pre-validated surveys can be understood by analyzing the underlying factors driving the scores among consumers (or customers) together by inferring the consumption or usage reports. Other industry and market reports can also be inferred on a case-by-case basis to support the analysis. A product manager or marketer should ask **'why'** if scores change during trend analysis for an existing product. For a new product launch, they should identify the factors driving these scores among consumers. This process can sometimes reveal the key shapers of the industry and the nuances of consumer perception and behavior within that sector.

REFERENCE AND SOURCE LITERATURE

REFERENCE

Ehrenberg, A.S.C. (2000) *Repeat buying: Facts, theory and applications.* Oxford University Press.
Lewis, E. St. Elmo (1898). *Financial Advertising.* New York: The Bankers Publishing Co.
Engel, J. F., Kollat, D. T., & Blackwell, R. D. (1968). *Consumer Behavior.* New York: Holt, Rinehart & Winston.
Engel, J.F., Blackwell, R.D. and Miniard, P.W. (1995) *Consumer Behavior.* 8th edn. Fort Worth: Dryden Press.

SOURCE LITERATURE

CX Today (no date) *What is CPaaS? A definition, use cases and top providers.* Available at: https://www.cxtoday.com/crm/what-is-cpaas-a-definition-use-cases-and-top-providers/ (Accessed: 25 October 2025).

Sprinklr (no date) *Customer journey: Understanding the modern CX landscape.* Available at: https://www.sprinklr.com/cxm/customer-journey/ (Accessed: 25 October 2025).

Harvard Business School Online (2025) *Mastering the Buying Journey: Key Stages & Examples. [online] Business Insights Blog.* Available at: https://online.hbs.edu/blog/post/buying-journey [Accessed 30 Oct 2025]

Halligan, B. and Shah, D. (2010) *Inbound Marketing: Get Found Using Google, Social Media, and Blogs.* Hoboken, NJ: Wiley.

MobileSquared Ltd (2024) *Trends In CPaaS: WhatsApp Business set to overtake SMS as CPaaS Providers' most trusted messaging channel,* 13 May. Available at: https://www.mobilesquared.co.uk/2024/05/13/whatsapp-business-set-to-overtake-sms-as-most-trusted-messaging-channel/ (Accessed: 25 October 2025).

Sprinklr (no date) *What is CCaaS?* Available at: https://www.sprinklr.com/blog/ccaas/ (Accessed: 25 October 2025).

The above references and source literature offer contextual insights into communication technology, industry evolution, and consumer engagement trends, which provide background for interpreting the *Market Romanticism* concept's application and usage

ABOUT THE AUTHOR

Shrivatsan Balagopal is the Founder and CEO of Neutralfone.

He is a venture builder and corporate entrepreneur with deep expertise in product management, strategy, and innovation. His experience spans corporate leadership and entrepreneurial ventures. He is a **knowledge contributor** to **CVMBoK** — the first-ever definitive guide to **Customer Value Management** in the **telecom** industry.

With over a decade of experience, Shrivatsan has co-built **IT-enabled service ventures**, founded a **wireless network and CCaaS startup,** and **led CPaaS product at Vodafone Idea** as **AGM – Product Management**.

His expertise **includes go-to-market strategy, productization, and commercialization** of solutions such as **Remote Tech Support, Fixed Wireless Access (FWA), Contact Center as a Service (CCaaS), Communication Platform as a Service (CPaaS),** and **AdTech** across **India, the United States, and other global markets**. He has also managed the **legal and regulatory complexities** of productization across multiple regions.

He is an **accredited arbitrator and dispute resolution practitioner,** with experience in **commercial and contractual disputes**.

Shrivatsan holds an **MBA from IIM Trichy**, a **PGDADR** from **NALSAR University of Law,** and a **B.Tech in Electronics and Communication Engineering from SRM Institute of Science and Technology,** Chennai, India.

Author : Shrivatsan Balagopal
Year of Publication: 2025
Copyright Registration No. LD- 20250170667
Paperback ISBN: 978-93-344-5030-9
Digital ISBN: 978-93-344-4551-0

www.marketromanticism.com

www.ingramcontent.com/pod-product-compliance
Ingram Content Group UK Ltd.
Pitfield, Milton Keynes, MK11 3LW, UK
UKHW020051200726
13845UKWH00056B/805

9 789334 450309